AUG   1999

ELECTRIC FISH

A TRUE BOOK

by
Elaine Landau

Children's Press®
A Division of Grolier Publishing
New York London Hong Kong Sydney
Danbury, Connecticut

Reading Consultant
Linda Cornwell
Learning Resource Consultant
Indiana Department
of Education

An electric eel

Visit Children's Press® on the Internet at: http://publishing.grolier.com

Library of Congress Cataloging-in-Publication Data

Landau, Elaine.
  Electric fish / by Elaine Landau.
    p.   cm. — (A True book)
  Includes bibliographical references and index.
  Summary: An introduction to various species of electric fish, particularly the electric eel, explaining how they generate and discharge electricity.
  ISBN: 0-516-20666-4 (lib. bdg.)   0-516-26491-5 (pbk.)
  1. Electric fishes—Juvenile literature. [1. Electric fishes.] I. Title.
II. Series.
  QL639.1.L27 1999
  597—dc21   98-16122
                                                                              CIP
                                                                              AC

GROLIER
PUBLISHING

Contents

Electric eels are among the best-known electric fish.

Electric Eels

You have probably heard that touching faulty, or damaged, wiring can give you a strong electric shock. But did you know that the same thing can happen if you touch an electric eel?

In spite of its name, this fish is not a true eel. However, its

The Amazon River Basin is the area surrounding the Amazon River. The Amazon is the world's second-longest river.

long, snakelike body makes it look like an eel. The electric eel is a freshwater fish found in parts of South America, such as the Amazon River Basin and the Orinoco River. It lives in the muddy creeks, lakes, and marshlands there.

People who live along lakes and rivers where electric eels can be found must be careful around these fish.

The electric eel is one of about five hundred different kinds of fish that are able to give off an electric current. Most people have been more interested in the electric eel because it releases a greater

The black ghostfish is an electric fish.

Can you imagine a fish with the ability to kill something as large as a horse?

amount of electricity than any other fish. The shock from an electric eel is powerful enough to kill a horse! This is a book about this unusual fish and some others like it.

An Interesting Fish

The electric eel is an interesting-looking fish. The largest ones grow up to 8 feet (2 meters) long. Young electric eels are an olive-brown color with light-yellow markings. But as they grow older, the markings disappear. The adults are olive-brown with

Young electric eels have light markings on their bodies (above). This picture (right) shows the orange throat area and small, beady eyes of the electric eel.

an orange throat area and green, beady eyes.

Most fish get all the oxygen they need from the water. But the electric eel also needs air to survive. It comes to the water's surface at least every fifteen minutes for a fresh supply of air. These fish live in muddy waters where there is little oxygen. If they couldn't get extra oxygen directly from the air, they would die in less than twenty minutes.

But how does a fish get oxygen from the air? Unlike

The muddy waters of the electric eel's habitat contain low amounts of oxygen.

humans, the electric eel does not have lungs for breathing. Instead, it has blood vessels in its mouth. These blood vessels take in oxygen when the fish pokes its head out of the water to gulp some air.

This is one important way the electric eel has adjusted to life in the low-oxygen waters of its habitat.

The electric eel has two small fins that help to keep it steady in the water. But it moves through the water with its long anal fin. This fin runs along the fish's underside from the end of its tail to its throat. It allows the fish to move freely in the water. An electric eel can move up, down, forward, or backward with equal speed and ease.

The electric eel's electrical organs are in its bulky back end and pointed tail. These

The organs responsible for delivering electric shocks are located in the back end and tail of the electric eel.

parts make up most of the eel's body. The fish's heart and other important organs are all in the front end. The front end makes up only a small portion of the electric eel's body. That explains how

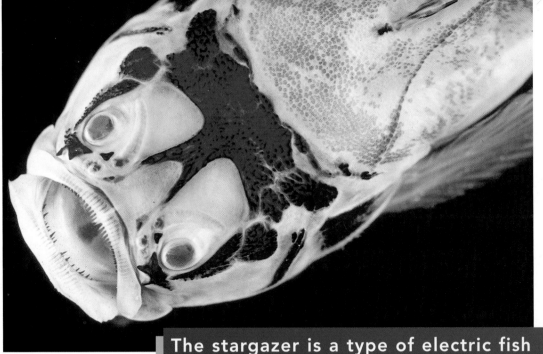

The stargazer is a type of electric fish that carries its electrical organs above its eyes. (In this overhead view of a stargazer skeleton, the white areas over the eyes are the electrical organs.)

most of an electric eel's body can be bitten off by a predator and it will still survive. Also, this fish heals rapidly. It is able to regrow any lost parts.

Fish such as the electric eel use their electrical powers to defend themselves when attacked by an enemy. They stun or kill prey, such as fish or frogs. They also use their electricity as a sort of radar system. By giving off a series of electric pulses, they can find objects and predators in the muddy water where it is difficult to see clearly.

The fish's electrical organs can deliver a powerful charge.

The electric eel can locate prey by sending a series of electrical signals through the water.

The fish has three pairs of electrical organs on each side of its body. Each organ is made up of a lot of small electrical cells. Although the

A resting electric eel does not give off electricity.

electric eel does not give off
electricity when it is at rest,
a low amount of electricity is
given off as soon as it starts
to move. At its strongest
level, an adult electric eel can

deliver an electric charge that can easily stun or kill its prey. However, the electric eel is not harmed by its own electrical discharge.

The electric eel gives off three to five bursts of electricity every time its electrical organs spring into action. Each burst lasts less than a second. In laboratory experiments, the eel's electricity has been strong enough to turn on a light bulb!

Can A Fish Swim Backward?

Electric eels scan prey similar to the way scanners work at a grocery store checkout.

An electric eel swims backward to reach its prey.

Yes. When an electric eel senses prey nearby, it swims past it a little. Then the eel swims backward to "scan" the prey with its electric pulse. Electric eels use this method because their poor eyesight means they can't easily see their prey.

Electric Eels As Pets?

Are you looking for an unusual pet? Are you thinking about getting an electric eel? If you are, think again. Many people enjoy viewing these fish in large public aquariums. But electric eels are rarely found in home aquariums.

These boys (left) are visiting an aquarium to view electric fish. Electric eels usually live alone in a tank (below).

There are several reasons. The electric eel cannot live in a tank with other fish because of its electrical discharges. It would not be long before most of the eel's tankmates would be stunned by its electrical charges—and then eaten. And two electric eels should not be kept together in the same tank. Fights break out and the eels bite each

Although these electric eels share one tank, keeping them together is not a good idea.

other and slap each other with their long tails. Each fish usually discharges enough electricity to injure the other.

People who handle electric eels must always be extremely careful. They need to wear thick rubber gloves for protection when they touch these fish. The electric eel's electrical discharge is so powerful that it is one of the few South American fish with no enemies besides humans.

Individuals who have tried to breed electric eels in aquariums mostly have been unsuccessful. This may be partly because these eels do not reach their full size in fish tanks. As a result, they cannot reproduce. Only a little is known about the electric eel's

This adult electric eel will not grow to its full size because it lives in an aquarium.

This young electric eel will grow to about 8 feet (2 meters) long.

breeding habits in the wild. During their breeding season, the electric eel disappears from its usual habitat. When it returns it brings its newborn young with it. These small electric eels are usually 4 to 6 inches (10 to 15 cm) long.

The Electric Catfish

While the electric eel may be the best-known electric fish, it is not the only one. There are many others, including the electric catfish and the electric ray.

The electric catfish is found in the waters of central Africa and the Nile Valley. It is the

The electric catfish is another well-known species of electric fish.

only catfish that has the ability to deliver an electric shock. Unlike many other catfish, the electric catfish has a plump body. Its electrical cells lie in a layer of fatty tissue beneath its skin. It is a gray-brown color with beige around its head and stomach. Its eyes are extremely small.

Although this is an electric catfish, not all catfish have electrical organs.

This catfish is about 12 inches (30 centimeters) long.

Electric catfish come in a variety of sizes—from about 3 inches (8 cm) to 4 feet (1 m) long. This fish rests in the water during the day and comes out at night to look for food. An electric catfish is not as powerful as an electric eel.

One electric catfish can give off several jolts of electricity in a row.

But a large electric catfish can give off a strong jolt of electricity that is followed by several smaller jolts.

Long ago, the electric catfish was used for medical purposes. In Africa, when a person complained of pain, a live electric catfish might be placed on the part of the patient's body that hurt. The electric shock that followed was believed to cure the person.

The ancient Egyptians greatly respected the electric catfish. Its picture has been found on Egyptian tombs and on the walls of buildings. On special days, an electric catfish might be cooked and eaten. Today, it is still eaten by people in some parts of Africa.

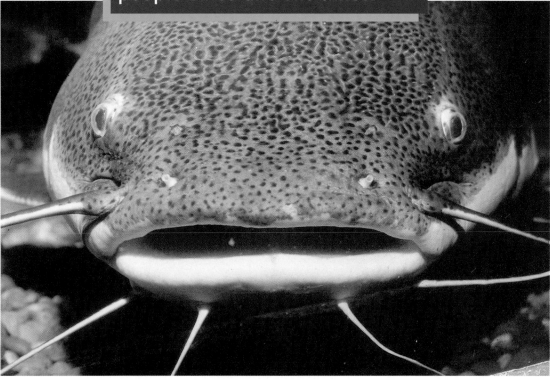

Electric catfish have fascinated people since ancient times.

Electric catfish are so fierce that only the very young can be kept in tanks with other fish. They eat almost anything that is available—from worms to fish.

Other Electric Fish

There are many other electric fish besides the ones you've seen so far. A few more examples include:

◄ The paddle-fish, which looks similar to a shark

The knifefish
▼

▲ The elephantnose fish

The Electric Ray

The electric ray is a flat, disk-shaped fish. More than thirty-five species of electric rays live in the tropical waters of the world. The smallest are less than 18 inches (46 cm) long. The largest grow up to 5 feet (2 m) long.

An electric ray at rest on the ocean floor

This fish has two large electrical organs on each side of its head just beneath the skin. It uses its electrical organs to escape from its enemies and to capture its prey.

Although electric rays do not produce as much electricity as electric eels, they can still stun their victims. They

The electrical organs are located on the sides of the electric ray's head, near its eyes.

The electric ray wraps its fins around its prey to bring it close to the electrical organs.

do this by wrapping their fins around their prey to place all of their electrical power in one spot.

The ancient Greeks and Romans were fascinated by the electric ray. Ancient doctors sometimes used the electric ray to treat patients who had headaches. The patient would hold the fish against his or her forehead.

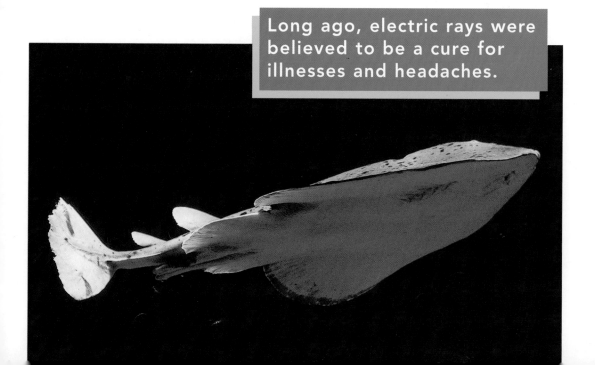

Long ago, electric rays were believed to be a cure for illnesses and headaches.

Today, there is no medical need for the electric ray. However, scientists continue to study them. And sometimes fishermen will accidentally

Scientists at an aquarium study a tank holding an electric fish.

All kinds of electric fish are likely to exist for thousands of years to come.

hook one. They get a jolt when they examine their catch. But that is to be expected with an electric fish!

To Find Out More

Here are some additional resources to help you learn more about electric fish and the oceans of the world:

 **Books**

Bailey, Donna. **Fish.** Raintree Steck-Vaughan, 1990.

Brenner, Barbara and Bernice Chardiet. **Where's That Fish?** Scholastic, 1994.

Cole, Joanna. **The Magic School Bus on the Ocean Floor.** Scholastic, 1992.

Doubilet, Anne. **Under the Sea from A to Z.** Crown Publishers, 1991.

Roberts, M. L. **World's Weirdest Sea Creatures.** Troll, 1993.

Snedden, Robert. **What Is a Fish?** Sierra Club Books For Children, 1993.

Organizations and Online Sites

Electric Catfish
*www.aquariacentral.com/
fishinfo/fresh/electric.htm*

This site contains more information about electric catfish.

Electric Fish
*www.bbb.caltech.edu/
bowerlab/ElectricFish/*

Here you'll find information and photographs of electric fish, with links to other sites.

**Fish and Wildlife
Reference Service**
5430 Grosvenor Lane
Suite 110
Bethesda, MD 20814

Fish Cam
www.netscape.com/fishcam/

See live pictures from a tropical fish aquarium and get links to other interesting sites.

Fish FAQ
*www.wh.whoi.edu/
homepage/faq.html*

Sponsored by the Northeast Fisheries Science Center, this site is full of fascinating facts about fish.

Important Words

breed to produce a particular type of animal

habitat surroundings, the place where an animal is found naturally

jolt a sudden shock

oxygen a colorless gas that is found in the air, humans and animals need oxygen to breathe

predator an animal that hunts other animals for food

prey an animal that is hunted for food

reproduce to create offspring or young

Index

Meet the Author

Elaine Landau has a Bachelor of Arts degree in English and Journalism from New York University and a Masters degree in Library and Information Science from Pratt Institute. She has worked as a newspaper reporter, children's book editor, and a youth services librarian, but especially enjoys writing for young people.

Ms. Landau has written more than one hundred nonfiction books on various topics. She lives in Miami, Florida, with her husband Norman and son, Michael.